A Polished Performan

Findings from NCVO's Leadership Programme for chief executives and chairs

Author: Tesse Akpeki
Editor: Marta Maretich

NCVO Mission Statement

NCVO's vision, mission and values

NCVO's vision

NCVO's vision is of a fair and open society, which encourages and is supported by voluntary action.

NCVO's mission

NCVO aims to:

- give a shared voice to voluntary organisations

- cultivate an environment that fosters their development

- help voluntary organisations to achieve the highest standards of practice and effectiveness

- provide leadership to the voluntary sector in tackling new issues and unmet needs.

NCVO's working values

NCVO will:

- reflect the priorities and needs of member organisations both in its services and policies

- provide services which are characterised by high quality, integrity and respect for recipients

- encourage voluntary organisations to learn both from each other and from wider best practice

- provide information in an open way with due regard to confidentiality

- reflect the diversity of the voluntary sector in its work

- provide continuing professional and personal development for its staff

- apply equal opportunities practice in its governance, services and as an employer.

Published by NCVO Publications.

National Council for Voluntary Organisations,
Regent's Wharf, 8 All Saints Street, London N1 9RL

© NCVO 2004

All rights reserved. No part of this publication may be reproduced or transmitted in any form or by any means, electronic, mechanical, photocopying, recording or otherwise, without the prior permission of the publisher.

Typeset by NCVO Publications.

Printed by Latimer Trend & Company Limited.

ISBN 0 7199 1623 2

Contents

Acknowledgements

Our thanks goes to the chairs and chief executives who generously gave of their time to participate in the Barclays Leadership Programme. Thanks goes to Emma King, Rebecca Forrester and to Peter Dyer who provided top quality support to the programme. Our masterclass leaders and keynote speakers, Lady Tumim, Stuart Etherington, Ben Kernighan, Dorothy Dalton, Michael Caudrey, Jane Slowey, Barbara Taylor, Peter Brinckerhoff, Linda Laurance, Dr Richard Goldbaum, Pesh Framjee, Dr Dame Karlene Davis and Carol Weisman.

Final thanks goes to Barclays PLC without whose support this qualitative leadership programme would not have been possible.

Introduction

Leaders in the voluntary sector have never been under more pressure. In organisations large and small, Chairs and Chief Executive Officers (CEOs) are working hard to keep up with the pace of regulatory change, answer calls for better governance and manage the complex relationships that underlie day-to-day operations. To help them meet these challenges, NCVO, with funding from Barclays, established the NCVO Leadership Programme in 2002. This unique programme offers an array of courses, workshops, master classes and one-to-one advisory sessions especially designed to address the needs of these key players. It also puts NCVO in direct contact with hundreds of top executives and Chairs and gives us an opportunity to hear their concerns.

Now, halfway through the Leadership Programme's three-year remit, a clearer picture is beginning to emerge of the hopes and fears of leaders today. This publications aims to capture this important data. It documents some of these concerns and analyses them in the light of support provision on the part of NCVO and other agencies. It addresses the questions: What issues most worry leaders? What help can they currently call on? And what can NCVO and other agencies do to better meet their current and future needs?

Where the information comes from

Most of the information in this publication derives from two sources. The first is a series of one-to-one interviews conducted by NCVO staff with CEOs and Chairs currently participating in the Leadership Programme. This relatively small but carefully selected group answered a series of probing questions designed to draw out their fears, frustrations, hopes and ambitions for themselves and the organisations they lead. To add to this data, we've brought together comments and ideas that have surfaced during our group master classes and round tables for leaders. In all cases, the participants were promised anonymity to allow them to speak their minds candidly about the most sensitive issues.

In all, we heard from around 500 CEOs and Chairs from a diverse range of organisations. In-depth interviews were held with a sample group of CEOs and Chairs (see *Our sample group* on page 4).

All sizes of organisation were represented in this sample from those with no staff at all to large multi-nationals. Our leaders came from a variety of backgrounds and had different levels of experience. They called themselves by various titles but for the sake of simplicity, in this publication we've chosen to call all the board leaders by the title of Chair and all the top executives by that of CEO.

Presenting the findings

Once the comments were in, we collated them and analysed them for common themes. We sought concerns that recurred in all kinds of contexts, ones felt across the sector regardless of organisational size, type or ethos. What we discovered was a set of issues that stood out in almost every exchange with sector leaders: concerns revolving around the big questions of effectiveness, accountability and governance practice. We broke the findings down into issues for Chairs, issues for CEOs and issues that were shared by both. By doing this, we hoped to draw attention to points where their concerns converged and where they diverged: both shed light on their respective governance roles and the challenges they face together and separately.

For convenience, we grouped our findings into several main areas. *What keeps them awake at night* addresses the most persistent worries of CEOs and Chairs, and examines the services they can call on for help. *What's on their minds* charts the current top concerns of CEOs and Chairs and provides a revealing analysis of their similarities and differences. *Handling relationships* gets at the knotty issues of organisational relationships while *Strategic challenges* documents what Chairs and CEOs believe to be the most important issues facing them in the near future. Taking a more specific focus, *Special cases* highlights the distinctive issues of small and membership organisations revealed by this survey. *Skills they need now* offers a bullet-point rundown of the top skills most leaders feel they need today – and lack. Finally, *What helps* charts some of the techniques CEOs and Chairs have tried successfully and *Top trends* gives a rundown of changes in the sector as we see them.

Broadening the conversation

Part of our aim in carrying out this survey was to flag areas where we, NCVO, can provide more support to leaders. With an eye to developing our own programmes, we've provided a needs analysis for each section that weighs the requirements of leaders against available support. Additionally, we've included some general recommendations for service provision, some that can be carried about by NCVO, others that may be relevant for other agencies. The purpose of these recommendations is mostly to address the issues raised by this survey on a practical level: What can be done to help these leaders? What do we need to do to give them the support they're asking for?

Another motivation for publishing our findings is simply to broaden awareness and encourage debate. All kinds of voluntary sector leaders, CEOs and Chairs alike, suffer from a sense of isolation, a feeling that they have no peers with whom to share their worries and from whom to get support.

We hoped to create a more inclusive conversation, to let others hear the voices of these individuals and to bring sometimes hidden issues into the light. By creating a climate of openness, NCVO hopes to draw more participants into this vital conversation about leadership – and so increase the chances of finding innovative solutions to difficult problems.

Our sample group

13 Chairs and 15 CEOs, 14 men and 14 women, from the following kinds of organisations:

- Professional support group
- Disability advocates
- Gay and lesbian group
- Children's organisation
- Legal support group
- Umbrella organisation
- Voluntary sector recruitment service
- Youth organisation
- Black organisation
- Training organisation
- Refugee/migrant organisation
- Environmental charity
- Sports organisation
- Educational support organisations
- International non-governmental organisations
- Networking organisations
- Student loan organisation
- Membership organisations

Chairs

Doing the job effectively

Many Chairs lacked confidence in their knowledge of their role and their skills. Many had no prior experience with chairing and received, at the time of their appointment, no proper induction or formal handover from the previous Chair. Few had any peer support in the form of someone to share problems with and seek solutions. They were left guessing as to whether they were doing the right things. Were their efforts adequate? Was it their fault if the board wasn't productive? Had they overlooked an essential task?

Needs: Chairs had many anxieties about their basic level of competency and some good resources already exist for them, others are being developed. Training in facilitation and meeting planning are available through organisations like NCVO, ACEVO and the Management Centre. NCVO also offers Chair inductions. A comprehensive guide for Chairs, like *The Good Trustee Guide*, plus a publication to help novice Chairs move more smoothly into the role are currently being developed by NCVO. Better publicity for existing resources would help more Chairs take full advantage and more networking would help more Chairs hear of the help available to them.

Managing conflicts

Many Chairs pointed to conflict as a source of anxiety. Chairs find themselves in the firing line, managing, mediating, trying to keep the peace in conflicts of all kinds: between the board and the CEO, between individual board members and factions. Indeed, they also see their own share of strife, frequently finding themselves involved in struggles with trustees and with the CEO. Many Chairs expressed the need for more support to deal with conflict.

Needs: Conflict was a huge issue for Chairs and one of the areas where they most felt the need for support. More availability of training in conflict management and facilitation, plus personal support through peer mentoring and coaching could ease the burden. The Centre for Effective Dispute Resolution (CEDR) currently offers good training courses in negotiation, mediation and conflict prevention and management. Some legal firms provide these services on a professional basis, but they can be costly. But making professional conflict resolution and mediation services more easily available to all types of organisations at affordable prices could go a long way toward helping Chairs solve these problems.

Meeting regulatory demands

Chairs felt that the regulatory buck for the organisation stopped with them and that they were ultimately responsible for their organisation's compliance with the law. Increasing regulation in all areas including charity regulation (which they realise is just about to undergo an overhaul) plus all the other kinds of regulation specific to their cause and activities: the Children's Act, the Disability Act, the Equal Opportunities Act and so on, kept them up at night wondering *Are we on top of things?* This was especially true for Chairs of organisations that work with children and other vulnerable groups. In a climate of increased scrutiny, loud calls for more accountability and harsher consequences for getting it wrong, the pressure, they felt, is really on.

Needs: Chairs of all types of organisations feel the strain of keeping up with regulatory demands. Those in the know rely on Charity Commission briefings and updates like those offered by NCVO and Sandy Adirondack. Some organisations take advantage of the free email update services offered by many large accountancy firms such as Baker Tilly, Deloitte & Touche, Kingston Smith and

KPMG. The information is out there, but more could be done to teach organisations where to go to get it. Many leaders of all sizes of organisations expressed the need for more detailed guidance to help them respond to new regulations. What exactly do they need to do in practical terms?

Overseeing resources

Resources human, material and financial, preoccupied Chairs in the small hours. They stare at the ceiling and wonder whether the money's being well-spent and well-maintained, whether fundraising efforts will produce enough cash flow, whether the physical assets of the organisation are properly insured and the human assets properly protected. Chairs in medium and small organisations especially lose sleep over these issues. Chairs in big organisations were more confident that they had staff that could manage, monitor, and generally take care of the business side of things. At the opposite end of the spectrum, some Chairs admitted their organisations completely lacked both systems for monitoring and the skills to know whether monitoring was being carried out properly. To make matters worse, many actually had to manage staff who manage resources. Such Chairs often feared they lacked the skills to offer guidance or detect areas of risk.

Needs: For Chairs, overseeing resources proves a source of worry. Better overall competency in Chairing skills and governance training helps Chairs feel confident that they can set up systems to provide good resource oversight. A Chair with good skills, moreover, enables the board and helps ensure it remains engaged in overseeing activities. Programmes are available in these areas from NCVO and others. However, more needs to be done to help Chairs learn to work with the strategic plan, gearing board activity into annual

reporting cycles and strategic aims, and so creating systems that allow them to monitor meaningfully.

An equally serious concern was the lack of financial skills among Chairs. Many come to the position without any business background at all and don't feel they would be able to spot a risk if they saw one. Chairs need more training in specific financial planning and management skills and The Charity Financial Directors Group can be a starting point for Chairs looking for ways to hone these skills. However, there are few financial courses tailored specifically for board leaders. Raising the awareness of the need for these skills among Chairs, then providing more opportunities for Chairs to obtain them early in their tenure, could help improve the quality of risk management throughout the sector.

Inevitably, Chairs in small organisations also supervise staff who in turn oversee resources (especially the CEO – see below). In such cases, both their lack of financial experience and their frequent lack of senior management training leaves them ill-equipped to judge the performance of staff members – or to know whether they are using resources correctly. Organisations like Capita Learning and Development (formerly part of the Industrial Society) offer good courses in HR management, but few are tailored to suit the special needs of Chairs. The Management Centre does offer sector-specific training and NCVO plans to review the possibility of working with other training organisations to develop more courses especially for Chairs. In the meantime, Chairs need access to professional external HR management support at affordable prices. Existing organisations offer some services, but again, most are not designed for voluntary sector organisations.

Supporting and supervising the CEO

This was a problem for Chairs in all organisations, rich and poor, large and small. CEOs tend to be highly skilled, often in areas where the Chair has little or no experience. For this reason, Chairs find it hard to line manage CEOs and don't know how to provide the right level of guidance or appropriate development opportunities. Many registered difficulty in knowing how close to get to the CEO, how much to share with him/her. This problem was echoed by the comments of CEOs, many of whom felt the lack of guidance and support from the Chair. It also finds expression indirectly in the troubles of Chair/CEO relationships (see below).

Needs: Many Chairs mentioned their uncertainty about being able to properly support and supervise the CEO. Some of the doubt arose from lack of clarity about roles which governance training for both parties can help. Another aspect of uncertainty arises from a more intractable source: a lack of expertise that would allow Chairs to understand and evaluate the work of the CEO. Chairs need access to external supervisors with the right skills and experience to oversee the top executive and offer advice about managing and developing him or her. ACEVO offers some services in this area but, judging from the level of concern we found among both Chairs and CEOs (see below), more needs to be done to address what looks like a significant gap in provision. Chairs (and, it emerges, CEOs as well) feel the need for much more support in this critical area. Based on the findings of this survey, NCVO is in the process of reviewing where investment could make a difference.

CEOs

Staying at the leading edge

CEO: 'I lie awake at night wondering what I'll do if I get up in the morning to find my ideas have all dried up.'

Most CEOs we spoke to expressed anxiety about staying ahead of the game. They spoke of how difficult it was to keep on top of the many aspects of their job: meeting regulatory demands, handling staff, working with the Chair and trustee board, keeping in touch with members and service users and fulfilling an ambassadorial role for the organisation in the community. Many expressed the wish for a more engaged trustee board or a wise, experienced Chair who could share some of the pressure. More commonly, CEOs said they felt isolated in their role and regretted the lack of professional development opportunities that could improve their performance and help them feel more competent.

Needs: Many CEOs in this survey registered the lack of sources of easily available, specific guidance and confidential advice for professionals in their position. What they wanted was not relationship counselling, they told us, but high quality information to help them solve their practical problems. They also wanted the opportunity to network with other CEOs and receive their advice and support. Peer networking, mentoring and coaching opportunities were welcomed by those lucky enough to find them. NCVO's master class series offered some of what CEOs were after but much more needs to be done to offer the highly specialised support required by these professionals. Again, as a result of the findings of this survey, NCVO is currently reviewing how best to provide for some of the voluntary sector's most influential leaders.

When the Chair becomes an obstacle...

CEOs of all types of organisations were concerned about their relationship with the Chair. Healthy relationships, although they do exist, are in the minority. Many CEOs thought of the Chair as a problem in one way or another. Troublesome Chairs took many guises:

- those who simply don't know their role or fail to carry out responsibilities
- dependent Chairs, usually new appointees, often doomed by short tenure to leave the job just as they've learned how to do it
- Chairs who don't understand CEO issues – or indeed the issues facing the organisation
- Chairs who don't wish to know the CEO or work cooperatively with him/her, believing any relationship compromises board integrity
- Chairs who circumvent the CEO and undermine him/her with staff
- long-serving Chairs who should go but won't.

Whatever form the problem with the Chair takes, the failure of this officer creates problems for the CEO. It muddies the waters between the CEO and the board and removes a vital channel of communication between the governing body and the executive. A weak Chair contributes to weakness in governance practice so that the board itself may function poorly or not at all. Undermining Chairs strip the CEO of his/her rightful authority and make it impossible for him/her to be effective. Clueless Chairs leave the CEO operating in a vacuum and fail to offer him/her needed support and development opportunities.

Needs: Problems with the Chair dogged CEOs in organisations of all sizes. Part of the answer lies with better support and training for Chairs (see above) including good Chair inductions in which the CEO participates. A clear understanding of roles and responsibilities on both sides goes a long way toward easing tension, but the time is ripe for more comprehensive guidelines on how to foster good CEO/Chair relations – perhaps from NCVO.

Both Chairs and CEOs would also benefit from the opportunity to participate jointly in professionally facilitated discussions that focus on sensitive issues that can't be resolved – or even discussed – effectively. NCVO and CEDR offer some services in this area, but one-to-one interventions are staff-intensive and expensive. Wider provision of accessible, affordable mediation and conflict resolution services would also help CEOs navigate difficult straits with their Chairs and move the organisation forward. Training in conflict prevention and negotiation for both parties could help, too. More opportunities to learn these skills would be welcomed by CEOs and Chairs alike.

Difficulty building a good management team

CEO: 'There are staff imposed on me who can't deliver the current agenda for the organisation but I can't get rid of them. How do I handle all the tensions surrounding this issue?'

A CEO comes into an organisation determined to bring needed change – only to find that the management team he/she must work with isn't up to the job. Staff may lack needed skills or the will to do things differently. Or they may simply be hostile to the CEO and his/her agenda. This, CEOs said, brought innovation in organisations to a screeching halt. No matter how good their plans, they could be scuttled by lack of staff competency. But when they try to get rid of staff, it creates conflict. They have trouble finding support for changes on the board. When they take it upon themselves to force an unproductive staff member out, they risk ending up in an employment tribunal.

Needs: The difficulty of getting the kind of staff they need comes up again and again in different forms in the CEO comments. To deal with this issue – which looks to become more acute in the near future (see Strategic challenges, page 19) – CEOs need to develop their strategic planning skills and their ability to link strategic goals clearly to recruitment and training programmes. They need to encourage more informed debate about staffing at the board level and to work with the trustee board to get backing for making staff changes.

Obviously, CEOs need to continue to receive up-to-date information about employment regulations, specific guidance about how the law affects their organisation and good HR advice that will keep them out of employment tribunals. There's quite a bit of help out there: NCVO, the Charity Commission, ACAS and Sandy Adirondack all have useful publications, websites and email update systems. Equality bodies like the Equal Opportunities Commission and the Commission for Racial Equality can offer guidance, too. However, CEOs need to be more aware of when they need to seek advice – and of where to go to get help when the time comes.

Both

The lack of an effective board

CEO: 'Often the organisation is effective despite an ineffectual trustee board – but it would be so much stronger if it had the benefit of an objective, independent, engaged governing body.'

Both CEOs and Chairs registered the problems that occur when the board isn't fulfilling its role. They all wanted boards that had good skills and were well-versed in their role, clued in to key issues and dedicated to the organisation. But many had boards that didn't measure up. Weak boards:

- didn't understand their own role
- lacked members with the right skills
- had lost touch with the issues facing the organisation
- were riven by conflict
- had too many members to govern effectively
- were dominated by strong individuals or powerful cliques
- meddled in staff matters.

Both CEOs and Chairs talked openly, sometimes despairingly, about why the failure of the board makes their respective jobs so difficult. A sick or ineffectual board is in no condition to make needed policy or carry out monitoring. It tends to focus on the wrong things and ignore the big issues, leaving the organisation vulnerable to a host of risks. And it fails to offer guidance to the CEO or create a governance framework to shape decisions in the rest of the organisation. Frequently, it stands in the way of efforts by others such as the CEO and Chair, to bring about change that could improve the long-term prospects of the organisation.

CEO: 'A passive board may be easy for the CEO to manage, but it doesn't really help when it comes to running the organisation.'

Needs: There is help for 'bad', 'troublesome' or ineffectual boards available in the form of a number of development programmes such as those offered by NCVO. Basic training in board responsibilities and roles can start even the least capable board on the road to becoming more effective and many organisations in this survey were taking advantage of these services. Appraisal and assessment programmes, which many of our interviewees were instituting in their organisations, help to pinpoint problems and create a climate of continual learning and improvement. A point made by both types of leaders is that the process is long and complicated and support is needed, both for leaders and for the board, at all points along the way. There are no quick fixes, though improvement is quickly felt and improves morale.

However, clued-up CEOs and Chairs who want to develop the board can still find themselves isolated. More needs to be done to encourage a climate in the sector that fosters both individual trustee and board development. Specific practical guidance on common problems would be enthusiastically welcomed, such as:

- persuading non-contributing or troublesome trustees to move on
- downsizing an over-large board
- getting the board to understand, back and design its activity around the strategic plan
- broadening the recruiting programme to increase board diversity and ensure the quality of future governing bodies.

Based on the views of participants in this survey, more needs to be done to address the acute problems in the boardrooms of many membership organisations. These organisations often have large, vocal bodies of members and this can be a mixed blessing. The members' desire to have their views represented directly leads them to seek places on the board. In the interests of inclusivity, the board expands to accommodate more members. The result is

an over-large, fragmented and undisciplined board that fails to govern adequately: trouble and conflict ensue.

These kinds of organisations (and there are many of them) desperately need guidance on how to engage the membership appropriately and get members' support for a more effective governance structure. NCVO is considering creating a guide especially for them that lays out good practice for establishing the right balance between the needs of members and the requirements of governance.

The presence of funders on the trustee board was another point of concern for many Chairs and CEOs. In many cases, funding organisations place representatives in the boardroom as a means of overseeing the use of funds. The Institute of Charity Fundraising Managers offers some useful guidance in this area, but more would be welcomed. There may also be a need for guidance written expressly for funders showing them alternative ways of exercising oversight on the way their money is spent.

Improving governance practice

A hot issue: many of the participants in this series of conversations were already undertaking governance reviews of one form or another in their organisations. Reviews could take the form of reassessing and revising the governing document or constitution, reviewing board and board committee structures or looking at management staff structures. Many were instituting systems of self assessment, codes of practice, codes of conduct and policies to address issues of accountability and decision-making. Some employed consultants to see them through the process. Others undertook the work themselves using publications and advice from organisations like NCVO. Many brought in professional trainers to provide support with key phases of the process.

NCVO was struck by how widespread the trend toward restructuring was among our interviewees. Why were they doing it? Why now? It was partly explained by the fact that this cross-section of CEOs and Chairs were self-selecting: all were part of the leadership programme and by definition they were individuals seeking ways to improve governance practice. More telling is the fact that a large percentage of the organisations involved in this survey are currently facing either rapid growth or some other kind of radical change. Many had faced some kind of crisis in the recent past. These events brought the leadership up against the shortcomings of existing structures and impressed upon them the need to seek support as they went through the difficult process of changing the fabric of the organisation.

Needs: Many participants commented that, while it was difficult to bring in changes to the governing document or management structures, it was more difficult still to effect those changes in the working practice of the board and the organisation. To respond to the challenge they need ongoing support and access to high-quality advice as they continue to introduce change in their organisations. Availability of affordable development and training opportunities for the board is essential for those wishing to improve standards in the boardroom and many organisations are taking advantage of existing programmes.

By contrast, more needs to be done for leaders working to overhaul structures at a management level. Organisations making the jump from small to medium-sized find themselves with a whole new layer of managers for which old structures can't provide enough support. Established organisations trying to improve efficiency find themselves unable to make staffing changes when needed. Both CEOs and Chairs lack adequate sources of guidance on how to realise strategic change at the level of staffing – and to do it in a way that is legal, fair and not divisive to the organisation or damaging to its morale.

Guarding the organisation's reputation

Both Chairs and CEOs worried about reputation in an era when, for voluntary sector organisations, a good name is often the most valuable asset they possess. Leaders know that bad press, scandals, negative rumours and public failures can result very directly in loss of face, loss of faith and loss of funding. Lack of control over the organisation's image lays them open to 'bad news stories' and these can affect morale, sow strife and impede fundraising. Their concerns also have to do with the ambassadorial role that both CEOs and Chairs fulfil in different ways – a role which frequently brings them into conflict with one another. The question is: Who should speak for the organisation in a given circumstance?

Needs: Although they expressed concern about dealing with the organisation's public face, many CEOs and Chairs didn't know what to do to protect their organisation against the various forms of reputational risk. Guidance on how to craft a good communications strategy for the whole organisation – one that includes the CEO, staff members, volunteers, the Chair, board officers and trustees – would be welcome. More mentoring and peer guidance opportunities could also offer leaders the support they need to deal with tricky situations involving public and press attention. NCVO has a role in delivering in both these areas, but other organisations, too, could contribute.

Fear of failure

Both CEOs and Chairs had this all-too-
human fear of failure in the general sense.
Believing in the organisation and its mission,
they feared that their own shortcomings
might cause the organisation to fail. They felt
a sense of responsibility to service-users and
members, and they feared for their own
professional reputations.

Needs: The best remedy for this fear is to
instil leaders with more confidence. By giving
them more of what they need, we can
improve practice and alleviate this fear. By
their own admission, they need:

- good information
- access to training and external
  expertise in the areas where their
  own skills aren't enough
- peer support in the form of
  networking, mentoring and coaching
  opportunities
- sector support in the form of agencies
  like NCVO that reach out to them
  and give them opportunities to share
  problems and get assistance.

What's on their minds

By tallying the issues mentioned by interviewees, we chart and compare some current concerns of CEOs and Chairs.

Chair

77%	Board communication
54%	Board recruitment
46%	CEO/Chair succession planning
38%	Managing and clarifying board expectations
38%	Terms of office
38%	Involving members

CEO

100%	Managing change and dealing with rapid growth
93%	Governance review process
67%	Strategic thinking and planning
40%	Diversity in governance
33%	Keeping up with issues
33%	Lack of clarity in board roles
33%	Membership issues
33%	Getting the board to recognise the need for change
33%	Board managing instead of governing
33%	Downsizing the board

Observations

Shared concerns: CEOs and Chairs shared concern over lack of clarity about roles and the distinction between governance and management. Membership issues and membership involvement also concerned both CEOs (33%) and Chairs (38%). We noted that the only shared areas of concern are not the ones at the top of the two lists.

Chair top issue: The top issue for Chairs was board communication (77%). This specific issue was not one of concern for CEOs, although a few did mention concerns, such as surfacing the issues and dealing with board expectations, which touch on the need for more effective communication.

CEO top issues: The overwhelming concern amongst CEOs, in one form or another, was the topic of managing change and dealing with rapid growth (100%). This concern did not receive any mentions by Chairs at all. Similarly, the CEOs' number two concern, the process of governance review (93%), was not mentioned by any of the Chairs in this survey. This surprised us, since we would have expected the Chairs to be driving an agenda for governance change, not the CEOs. However, Chairs did raise concerns such as 'terms of office' and 'involving members' and these are perhaps some of the specific issues that a governance review may address.

One-sided issues: Board recruitment was important to Chairs (54%) in this survey but not to CEOs. By contrast, diversity in governance was on the minds of CEOs (40%) but, interestingly, not so far a concern for Chairs. 46% of Chairs were concerned about succession planning. CEOs didn't count this among their own concerns, but they did take an interest in who would succeed as Chair.

Trouble on board: Not surprisingly, dealing with problem trustees turned out to be more a concern for Chairs than it was for CEOs. Yet 'Getting the board to recognise the need for change', 'board managing instead of governing' and 'downsizing the board', each of which 33% of our CEOs mentioned as a concern, all point to problems with the board and with handling difficult members.

Handling relationships

The Chair/CEO relationship

CEO: 'In my 15 years of service to the same organisation I've seen five Chairs come and go. When individual Chairs proved difficult, I just put things on hold and waited for them to move on.'

A hot topic for Chairs and CEOs alike in all kinds of organisations; relationships between these two key players had issues on two fronts. First and most commonly, CEOs and Chairs clashed on the level of personality. The two types of leaders commonly had very different backgrounds, different styles and different priorities. They frequently tread on one another's toes – often unintentionally. Some fought openly for dominance. Others tolerated or avoided their opposite number, waiting for the day when he or she would simply move on – or die. When nothing was done to ease the tension between these two influential figures, personality clashes could lead to serious governance and morale problems for the organisation.

Roles – and the lack of a clear understanding of what they are – form the basis of the second set of CEO/Chair issues. Interestingly, NCVO has found that what first looks like a personality clash between leaders often turns out to have its roots in confusion about roles. Chairs and CEOs frequently got in one another's way. Many Chairs and CEOs complained that their opposite number sometimes acted in ways that were meddling, undermining or obstructive. Usually the trouble was characterised by lack of clarity as to who should be in the driver's seat in a given situation. CEOs wished aloud for a Chair that could facilitate a productive relationship with the trustee board while keeping to his/her side of the fence. Chairs expressed doubt about how closely they should work with the CEO. Questions arose from both Chairs and CEOs about what a good working relationship should look like. What was appropriate? What was good governance? What worked?

CEOs frequently said they wished the Chair would have more understanding of the issues they faced as top executives. And they felt that if they as CEOs had a clearer idea of how the board worked, they could provide more support and motivation. Overall, Chairs and CEOs who held regular meetings got along better. What was needed, some participants said, was a relationship that was supportive but 'not cosy', one in which both parties could speak their minds, share concerns and be 'critical friends'. The majority of interviewees were not sure how to arrive at this ideal state of affairs.

Needs: More work needs to be done to help Chairs and CEOs get this pivotal relationship right on both fronts. When a personality clash cripples the leadership, CEOs and Chairs need outside help in the form of affordable mediation and conflict resolution services. Professionally facilitated sessions in which quarrelling CEOs and Chairs can air issues and seek answers could help, too. Many of the leaders we spoke to were not aware that such services were available or felt their organisation could not afford them. Others had organisations in which the idea of getting help from the outside in such a sensitive area was an anathema. More publicity about such services and what they can achieve would lead more organisations to seek help before the situation gets critical. Peer networking, coaching and support schemes such as those offered by NCVO's leadership programme, can also give individuals a way to move beyond conflict.

Better role training can go a long way toward establishing a healthy CEO/Chair relationship from day one. Good inductions for both kinds of leaders are essential as are job descriptions and person specifications for both positions. Clear-cut protocols for raising issues and airing grievances help avoid CEO/Chair relationships going sour in the first place. To improve existing relationships, self-assessments for both parties can lead to a clearer sense of where problems lie and where solutions might be sought – they also provide an opportunity to revisit role issues. NCVO and other training organisations already provide some of what is needed in this area, but more could be done. The time seems right for comprehensive guidance on how to establish an appropriate and productive CEO/Chair relationship and NCVO is currently looking into what form this may take.

The trustee board

The problem of 'bad' or ineffectual boards came up again and again in these interviews for both types of leader. A weak, divided or combative board made difficulties for both Chairs and CEOs in different ways.

Needs: Relationship problems with the trustee board generally grew out of confusion about roles: What is the proper role of the board in the organisation? What is the correct relationship of the board to the Chair, CEO and staff? More training on roles and responsibilities for trustees plus a strong trustee code of conduct, meticulously enforced, can go a long way toward solving some relationship problems. Generally raising the awareness and skill level of boards was seen, by those who had implemented trustee training in their organisations, as a step toward improving relationships.

Staff

A frequent source of irritation for both Chairs and CEOs: staff relations become an issue when trustees, the Chair, funders or others interfere in managerial matters, ignoring the proper channels and attempting to exert direct influence on staff activity. This works in both directions: it was equally a problem when staff members bypassed established procedures and brought grievances directly to trustees or the Chair.

Needs: Again, a strong code of conduct, both for trustees and staff members, that spells out the proper method of bringing issues to the attention of staff and the trustee board.

Funders

Both CEOs and Chairs registered the delicacy of funder relationships and the challenge in keeping them positive. Many organisations had funders sitting on the board and they found this presented problems when it came to making decisions. Others struggled to shape their programmes to meet the expectations of funding bodies. Overall there was discomfort about the funder/charity relationship when it came to governance issues: How much influence should funders have over the way the organisation is run? What form should their involvement take?

Needs: Some guidance on how to work with funders already exists, but more could be done to help both funders and charitable organisations make the most of what should be a productive partnership. Trustee boards must learn how to guard the organisation's mission and vision even while actively seeking funding. Good procedures, such as monitoring that clearly shows the outcome of programmes, help boards satisfy funders while remaining firmly in the driver's seat. Strong strategic direction and consistent adherence to mission keep organisations on track and impresses potential funders at the same time.

For their part, funding bodies need to learn to recognise the value of quality governance and to put money behind developing the board and management. In the United States, progressive charities like the Rockefeller Foundation and the Mott Foundation provide funding specifically for such activities as CEO recruitment and board development. More could be done to encourage funders to use their money to engage with organisations in a way that will really make a difference to performance.

Members

CEO: 'There is nothing as powerful as a member who brings the voice of his or her experience into the boardroom.'

Member relations – and their effect on governance – turned out to be one of the surprise issues of this survey. The complex problems of trustee governance turn out to be even more complex in membership organisations. Both CEOs and Chairs registered the difficulty of engaging the membership productively while protecting the governance process. Leaders want to know how to tap into the expertise and experience of members without sacrificing their long-term strategic focus. They also wondered how to separate the issue of service delivery – obviously, the prime concern of most members – from larger governance issues. The basic question for leaders is: How do we square our democratic ideals, the sincere wish to represent the views of members, with the need to provide effective leadership?

Needs: As mentioned before, NCVO feels that it has heard a loud call for guidance on how to strengthen governance in membership organisations. It is currently reviewing its role in this area.

Special cases

Our survey showed how many issues voluntary sector leaders had in common regardless of the size, type or location of their organisation. However, CEOs and Chairs in small organisations and organisations with a membership base often faced different challenges and had different training needs.

Small organisations

Issues

- Managing and supporting staff – particularly when there is no other dedicated HR staff
- Managing staff performance and recruitment
- Dealing with staff disciplinary matters
- Maintaining a productive relationship with the community
- Finding the best role for individuals
- Tackling the 'founder syndrome' on the trustee board
- Delivering to the community.

What helps

- Good information
- The time and opportunity to do 'blue sky', creative thinking
- Using staff
- Finding funding that will pay for consultant services.

Membership organisations

Issues

- Governance reviews/constitutional change – or the need for them
- Making a board of trustees/members work effectively
- Recruiting the right people for the trustee board
- Systems for appointing or electing new trustees
- Public relations and communication with membership
- Motivating and engaging members in a productive way
- Accommodating local, regional and national differences
- Creating a healthy relationship between national and local bodies.

What helps

- Use of job descriptions and role training
- Board appraisal
- Constitutional changes
- Away days
- Good trustee induction.

Skills they need now

CEOs

- Understanding the broad financial picture
- Negotiation: contracts, funders, consultants
- Thinking, planning and acting strategically
- Managing people and motivating staff, particularly the staff directly below them
- Being effective in their ambassadorial role, dealing with the media, the public, funders, leaders, ministers
- Analysis: making sense of complex information
- For service delivery organisations: reading the outside environment accurately.

Chairs

- Motivating trustees and making the best use of their skills
- Mediation and conciliation skills
- Meeting facilitation skills
- Analysis skills that will help them understand what happens at meetings
- Leading the CEO recruitment process
- Understanding financial statements and being able to spot areas of risk
- Thinking strategically, getting the board to understand and own the strategic plan.

Both

- General business and planning skills
- Leadership skills tailored to their particular role, their particular organisation
- Managing diversity of all kinds: gender, religious, ethnic, age
- Meeting regulatory requirements and creating a good environment in their organisations, avoiding trouble, building trust, creating a healthy balance.

Strategic challenges

A shortage of skilled staff

Both CEOs and Chairs registered the increasing difficulty of attracting and retaining staff with the right skills, especially top-level staff. More competition from the better-paid private sector, coupled with a shortage of individuals who combine hard skills with experience of the voluntary sector, means that it's harder to fill positions with the calibre of professional they'd like. Top quality CEOs and high-level managers were in particular demand by organisations – and were particularly hard to come by and hard to keep. This trend is set to increase as the sector becomes more professional and the pressure to recruit good, skilled people increases.

The challenge is to improve recruitment and development opportunities, and to motivate staff to believe in the mission enough to stay with the organisation rather than selling their skills elsewhere. Organisations need to devote more money to recruitment and development, not just for staff. The board, too, needs skill training as well as development to help them understand staffing issues and support change. Unfortunately, cash-strapped organisations tend to cut the training budget first – and suffer the consequences of high turnover and skill loss to other organisations and other sectors.

Competition from other sectors

Many participants noted that service provision organisations now face more then just the challenges presented by the mission. They have to compete for funding and sometimes for projects with other voluntary and private organisations. This means that they need better business skills and advice and getting it can sometimes prove difficult, requiring a new approach, a change in the culture of the organisation to respond to this new reality.

More diversity

The world is changing. Minority groups of all kinds are more participatory and more vocal in our society and new regulations require all kinds of organisations to treat individuals fairly and consistently. It is not just about race: age, sexual orientation and disability are all factors. But this is not just political correctness. It is a profound cultural shift that is already being felt at all levels of many voluntary organisations. Many CEOs and Chairs in our survey were trying to make sense of this new reality and the regulation that comes with it. Some are recruiting new kinds of trustees and tapping into a membership that reflects diversity. Others are reaching out to a broader spectrum of the community or offering new services that meet the needs of specific groups. Still others have yet to see what this change will mean for them, but most feel it will bring change in the way they operate.

Recruiting and retaining trustees

In a commercial world, fewer and fewer of us seem willing to do anything for free. Organisations are finding it ever more difficult to attract the kind of trustees that will give its governing body the energy it needs. Although more organisations are investing in governance training and trying to improve, there is still a long way to go to making trusteeship an attractive prospect. More effort needs to be made to cultivate good candidates and to offer serving trustees the opportunity to learn new skills and develop themselves. Organisations may not be able to offer cash, but they will need to think about other rewards they can offer: training, experience, personal development.

What helps

Both CEOs and Chairs had opinions about what helped them fulfil their roles more effectively. Here are the top techniques mentioned by participants in our survey.

Chairs

77% Use of job descriptions

77% Strengthening board development programme

61% Board networking/networking at meetings

61% Knowing where to go for help

46% Board appraisal

38% Selecting the right external advisors/consultants for board development work

38% Constitutional changes

38% Succession planning

CEOs

67% Knowing where to go/who to talk to for help

67% Addressing management and governance issues at a strategic level

53% Using the board as a resource

53% Good professional facilitation

40% Good decisions/effective action brought about by a clear understanding of the issues

Observations

Getting help: Both Chairs (61%) and CEOs (67%) thought that being able to speak to others and knowing where to get information were important. This seems to uphold the view that it's lonely at the top and CEOs and Chairs alike need someone to share pressures with. Networking and mentoring were mentioned by both kinds of leaders. While these were mentioned in NCVO's 1991 report *On Trust*, we have seen a much greater understanding of the benefits of these techniques in this survey.

Using professionals: Both types of leaders agreed on the importance of being able to seek help outside the organisation. Chairs saw this in the light of hiring professionals to assist with key stages of board development work (38%) while CEOs thought in terms of professional facilitation (53%). Many CEOs and Chairs talked of using outside consultants to manage all kinds of change in their organisations and this corresponds with NCVO's impression of an increase in the practice of seeking professional help throughout the sector. NCVO's publication *Getting Value from Consultants* aims to help organisations make good choices in this area.

Addressing big issues: CEOs talk of the benefit of addressing management and governance issues on a strategic or systemic level (67%). Chairs tend to see this in more narrow focus and talk of using job descriptions to help clarify roles (77%).

Note the difference

- 77% of the Chairs we spoke to rated board development programmes as very helpful to improvement. No CEO mentioned them, though they did register the problems caused by inefficient boards.
- 46% of Chairs thought board appraisals were a boon. Only a few CEOs even mentioned them – not enough to make the chart. However, CEOs did like the things that came out of appraisals such as clarity about roles and responsibilities, better teamwork and improved governance practice.
- Encouragingly, 53% of CEOs said that using the board as a resource has proved helpful. Chairs, by contrast, did not mention the CEO as a source of help. Maybe support from the CEO was simply assumed. Given that CEOs wanted greater clarity in how their boards could be motivated and supported, this indicates an area of concern.
- 38% of Chairs mentioned that constitutional changes and succession planning were helpful. No CEOs remarked on these.

Top trends

- Structural review of governance, management or both by all kinds of organisations
- Establishment of appraisal systems for CEO, Chair and trustee board
- CEOs and Chairs alike seeking ways to end isolation, find peer and other support
- Increased interest in mediation and conflict resolution services
- CEOs having difficulty finding high-level development opportunities
- Governance difficulties for membership organisations
- Human Resource difficulties for small voluntary organisations and community groups.

Give us your feedback

This conversation is ongoing – and so is the NCVO Leadership Programme. Our aim is to involve the widest possible spectrum of the voluntary sector community in this discussion of leadership today. If you have an interest in the issues raised in this publication call, email or write to us to let us know your views. Or simply fill out the attached *Leadership questionnaire* on page 29 and return it to us (address on the back cover of this publication).

Useful resources and support

National Council for Voluntary Organisations (NCVO)

The National Council for Voluntary Organisations (NCVO) works with and for the voluntary sector in England by providing information, advice and support and by representing the views of the sector to government and policy-makers.

The trustee and governance team at NCVO is dedicated to improving the effectiveness of voluntary sector organisations by strengthening their governing boards and enhancing the skills of trustees who sit on them.

NCVO offers a unique personalised development programme designed to help voluntary sector leaders perform more effectively. Supported by Barclays PLC, the NCVO Leadership Programme for Chief Executives and Chairs offers a range of training options to meet diverse needs.

www.ncvo-vol.org.uk
HelpDesk: 0800 2 798 798
www.askNCVO.org.uk
helpdesk@askncvo.org.uk

Advisory, Conciliation and Arbitration Service (ACAS)

ACAS aims to improve organisations and working life through better employment relations.

www.acas.org.uk
Tel: 08457 47 47 47

Association of Chief Executives of Voluntary Organisations (ACEVO)

ACEVO represent third sector leaders and provide them with support, advice and development opportunities.

www.acevo.org.uk
Tel: 0845 345 8481

American Society of Association Executives

Based in Washington in America, ASAE is the largest organisation of association executives and industry suppliers in the world. ASAE also serves as the international secretariat of the Global Forum of Societies of Association Executives, a global network for the association management profession worldwide.

www.asaenet.org

Action with Communities in Rural England (ACRE)

ACRE is a national charity whose purpose is to support sustainable rural community development.

www.acre.org.uk
Tel: 01285 653477

BoardSource

BoardSource, formerly the National Center for Nonprofit Boards, is based in America. It provides resources including practical information, tools and best practices, training, and leadership development for board members of nonprofit organisations worldwide.

www.boardsource.org

Board Builders

Board Builders is a company, based in America but which works internationally, dedicated to helping non-profits reach a higher level of success, and to help board and staff achieve greater joy in their work.

www.boardbuilders.com

Charities Aid Foundation (CAF)

CAF is an international non-governmental organisation providing specialist financial services to charities and their supporters.

www.cafonline.org

Capita Group

Capita learning and development – previously part of The Industrial Society.

www.capita-ld.co.uk
Tel: 0870 400 1000

Cass Business School, City University, London

Offering a range of qualifications relevant to voluntary sector leaders.

www.cass.city.ac.uk
Tel: 020 7040 8600

Centre for Effective Dispute Resolution (CEDR)

CEDR's mission is to encourage and develop mediation and other cost-effective dispute resolution and prevention techniques.

www.cedr.co.uk
Tel: 020 7536 6000

Charity Finance Directors' Group (CFDG)

The Charity Finance Directors' Group is a membership organisation set up in 1987 which specialises in helping charities to manage their accounting, taxation, audit and other finance related functions.

www.cfdg.org.uk
Tel: 020 7793 1400

Charities Evaluation Services (CES)

CES helps members of voluntary and community organisations to develop their own approaches to enhancing the quality of their services.

www.ces-vol.org.uk
Tel: 020 7713 5722

Charity Commission

The Charity Commission is established by law as the regulator and registrar for charities in England and Wales.

www.charitycommission.gov.uk
Tel: 0870 333 0123

Charity Trustee Networks

Charity Trustee Networks helps set up and provides support to networks of charity trustees.

www.trusteenetworks.org.uk
Tel: 01482 682252

Companies House

Companies House incorporates and dissolves limited companies; examines and stores company information delivered under the Companies Act and related legislation; and makes this information available to the public.

www.companieshouse.gov.uk
Tel: 0870 33 33 636

Directory for Social Change (DSC)

DSC help voluntary and community organisations to thrive through advice on: how to raise the money they need; how to manage their resources to maximum effect; how to influence the right people; what their rights and responsibilities are; and how to plan and develop for the future.

www.dsc.org.uk
Tel: 020 7391 4800 (London office)
Tel: 0151 708 0117 (Liverpool office)

Ethnic Minority Foundation

The Ethnic Minority Foundation (EMF) is committed to extending opportunities to people from ethnic minority communities throughout the UK.

www.ethnicminorityfund.org.uk
Tel: 0800 652 0390

Foundation for Good Governance

The Foundation for Good Governance works with boards to raise standards and improve practice; increases understanding of governance by research; and shares models of good governance. See also 'Governance Works'.

www.governance-works.org.uk
Tel: 0191 232 6942

Governance Institute

Based in America, the Governance Institute conducts research studies, tracks healthcare industry trends, and showcases the best practices of leading healthcare boards across the country.

www.governanceinstitute.com

Governance Works

www.governance-works.org.uk
Tel: 0191 232 6942

Independent Sector

Based in America, Independent Sector is committed to strengthening, empowering, and partnering with nonprofit and philanthropic organisations in their work on behalf of the public good.

www.independentsector.org

Institute of Chartered Secretaries and Administrators (ICSA)

ICSA is the professional body for Chartered Secretaries. A Chartered Secretary is qualified in company law, accounting, corporate governance, administration, company secretarial practice and management.

www.icsa.org.uk
Tel: 020 7580 4741

Institute of Chartered Accountants in England and Wales

The Institute of Chartered Accountants in England and Wales is the largest professional accountancy body in Europe.

www.icaew.org.uk
Tel: 020 7920 8100

Institute of Fundraising

The Institute of Fundraising promotes the highest standards of fundraising practice.

www.institute-of-fundraising.org.uk
Tel: 020 7627 3436

The King's Fund

Education Leadership Development at the King's Fund runs a wide range of courses to help managers and health professionals to develop leadership skills.

www.kingsfund.org.uk
Tel: 020 7307 2582

The Management Centre

The Management Centre run management and fundraising training programmes all over the UK and overseas. It also offers management and fundraising consultancy services.

www.managementcentre.co.uk
Tel: 020 7978 1516

McKinsey

McKinsey offer free registration for an email update service for a range of topics.

www.mckinsey.com

National Association of Councils for Voluntary Service (NACVS)

NACVS is the network of over 300 Councils for Voluntary Service (CVS) throughout England.

www.nacvs.org.uk
Tel: 0114 278 6636

NHS Leadership Centre

The NHS Leadership Centre was established in April 2001 to promote leadership development across the service.

www.modern.nhs.uk
Tel: 0845 600 0700

Nonprofit Governance & Management Centre

Based in Australia, the Nonprofit Governance & Management Centre have a firm commitment to quality management in the nonprofit sector which they believe starts with effective governance.

www.governance.com.au

Open University Business School

The Open University Business School is the largest business school in Europe and the largest MBA provider in the world.

www.open.ac.uk/oubs
Tel: 08700 100311

Roffey Park

Roffey Park offers executive education, with a focus on Leadership, People Management, Personal Effectiveness, Human Resources and Organisational Development.

www.roffeypark.com
Tel: 01293 854 059

Sandy Adirondack

Sandy Adirondack is a freelance management consultant and trainer working exclusively in the voluntary/not-for-profit sector.

www.sandy-a.co.uk
Tel: 020 7232 0726

Voluntary Sector National Training Organisation (VSNTO)

The Voluntary Sector National Training Organisation (VSNTO) supports workforce learning and development for paid staff, volunteers, management committee members and trustees within the voluntary and community sectors.

www.voluntarysectorskills.org.uk
Tel: 020 7713 6161

The Work Foundation (previously part of The Industrial Society)

The Work Foundation exists to inspire and deliver improvements to performance through improving the quality of working life. Previously part of The Industrial Society.

www.theworkfoundation.com
Tel: 0870 165 6700

Helpful publications

ACEVO

www.acevo.org.uk/main/publications.php?content=pubcatalog

- *Appraising the chief executive: A guide to performance review*
  Price £12.50

- *Leading the organisation: The relationship between Chairs and Chief Executives*
  Price £12.50

- *Partners in Leadership: A new style of governance and management for charities*
  Price £12.50

- *Talent rises to the top? Remuneration Survey 2003/04*

BoardSource

www.boardsource.org/Bookstore.asp

- *Leadership roles in nonprofit governance*
  Price $15.00

- *How to help your board govern and manage less*
  Price $15.00

- *Chief Executive Succession Planning*
  Price $52.00

- *The Board Savvy CEO*
  Price $28.00

- *Assessment of the Chief Executive*
  Price $65.00

- *Hiring the Chief Executive*
  Price $36.00

- *The Board Chair Handbook*
  Price $45.00

- *Chief Executive Compensation*
  Price $15.00

NCVO

http://shop.ncvo-vol.org.uk

- *Leadership Leadership Leadership*
  Margaret Bolton and Meg Abdy
  Published July 2003 by **NCVO** and **ACEVO**
  Paperback, 56 pages
  ISBN 1 900685 17 5
  £9.99 (£7.99 for **NCVO** and **ACEVO** members*)

- *Good Governance Action Plan*
  Sandy Adirondack
  Published 2002
  Paperback, 20 pages
  ISBN 0 7199 1545 7
  Price £10.00 (£8.00 **NCVO** members*)

- *Best Behaviour*
  Tesse Akpeki
  Published 2004
  Paperback, 29 pages
  ISBN 0 7199 1646 1
  Price £7.50 (£6.00 **NCVO** members*)

- *Living Policy*
  Published 2004
  Paperback, 70 pages
  Price £7.50 (£6 **NCVO** members*)
  ISBN 0 7199 1634 8

- *Setting Chief Executive Officer Remuneration*
  Tesse Akpeki
  Published 2001
  Paperback, 20 pages
  ISBN 0 7199 1582 1
  Price £12.50 (£10.00 **NCVO** members*)

> *To find out more about **NCVO** membership visit the **NCVO** website: **www.ncvo-vol.org.uk**

Leadership Questionnaire

The information provided in this form will be treated confidentially.

Address and contact details

Your role

CEO ☐   Chair ☐

Other (please specify)

_____

_____

_____

Questions about your organisation

Size (based on annual income):

Less than £100,000	☐
£100,000 - £500,000	☐
£500,000 - £1million	☐
£1million - £5million	☐
Over £5million	☐

Please indicate the nature of your activities by selecting the activity which is most important for your organisation

Religion	☐	unions	☐
Health	☐	Environment and animal welfare	☐
Social Services	☐	Education, employment, training and research	☐
Equality of opportunity, law and advocacy	☐	Resource and umbrella organisations	☐
Economic development, housing	☐	Other (please specify)	
International activities	☐		
Culture and recreation	☐		

_____

_____

_____

Business and professional associations,

Main aims or your organisation

Please sum up the main aims and objectives of your organisation, including the purpose for which it was established

Governance structure

How many trustees do you have?

Do you have a membership?

Do you have any committees that serve the board? If so, how many do you have, and what function do they perform (eg human resources, audit, etc).

_____

_____

_____

_____

Is your organisation...

An unincorporated association?	☐
A trust?	☐
A company limited by guarantee?	☐
An Industrial and Provident Society?	☐
Other (please specify)	

What about your current role or the current situation of your organisation worries you at the moment?

Governance review (eg restructuring)	☐
Membership issues (eg engagement)	☐
Board conflict	☐
Strategic planning or thinking	☐
Succession planning for CEO or Chair	☐
Board recruitment	☐
Board assessment of appraisal	☐
Chair support	☐
CEO support	☐
Other (please specify)	

What would you find helpful?

Peer mentoring   ☐

Networking   ☐

Coaching   ☐

Updates   ☐

Other (please specify)

Would you like to receive any more information from the Trustee and Governance Team at NCVO by joining our mailing list?

Yes ☐   No ☐

Thank you for completing this form.

If you have any enquiries, don't hesitate to contact the Trustee and Governance Team at trustee.enquiries@ncvo-vol.org.uk, on 020 7713 6161 or at Regent's Wharf, 8 All Saints Street, London N1 9RL.